PRAISE FOR

"Laura Di Franco's poems ~~appropriately~~ multi-tiered ruminations on the heart. Her work states what many of us (come on-admit it) whisper to ourselves on semi-empty subway cars, or to the moon. Bravery in and of itself does not, of course, guarantee successful poetic ruminations. Here the aforementioned courage and lyricism serves her work the way a richly lyrical motif enhances a symphony (and seduces the reader). Dive in to this volume headfirst. You'll be glad you did."

–Reuben Jackson, Author of Scattered Clouds

"Laura Di Franco puts shame to body shaming yourself and fire on the desire to be beautiful in her book: Warrior Desire, Love Poems to inspire Your Fiercely Alive Whole Self. Asking questions like, "What would it feel like to surrender to your deepest desires?" And "When was the last time you played?" The encouragement to discover your whole self: mind, body and spirit is evident in these pages committed to love as an adjective, noun, and verb. Laura uses her experiences as a love poem to inspire us all to heal through love of love, love of self, and love for others. This body of work is truly for the hopeful romantics, because it is evident here that Love is never Hope-Less."

–KaNikki Jakarta, Poet Laureate of Alexandria, Virginia

"So many of us not only lose our passion along the way, but we forget it even matters. Laura reminds us that indeed, it not only matters, but is what brings us back to life and fuels the deep fire within. Through her intimate poetry, personal reflections, and meaningful questions, she invites us to remember again. She invites us to ignite our fires again. "What do you live for?" "What thoughts keep you from speaking your heart out loud?" Good stuff for anyone feeling the call to awaken once more. "

–Terri St. Cloud, Bone Sigh Arts

"A box of chocolate dipped poems with raspberry song filling and a hint of chili pepper sprinkled over the top." That's how I would describe Laura Di Franco's book, *Warrior Desire Love Poems to Inspire Your Fiercely Alive Whole Self.* Each poem gently and sweetly de-robes the reader of their desire-restricting inhibitions leaving them naked yet unashamed. Lines like, "Rest your body down on my soul" shot up from the page and into my ear like a familiar melody I never heard before. The voice of her poems is hypnotic forcing you to make direct eye contact with your deepest desires and as she put it in her poem, *Make It Real,* "...[m]ove your love from your heart to your tongue."

Di Franco's poems will set your heart a glow with love thirsty flames as she speaks to the desperate, daring and audacious nature of what it means to be in love. She baptizes the reader in the *sometimes* turbulent waters of affection, infatuation and passion all while tenderly elevating the reader to their own freeness and authenticity.

In addition to being a poetic exploration of intimacy, sexual healing and untamed love, it also serves as the ultimate permission slip to unapologetically love fearlessly and be loved fiercely."

–Dinahsta "Miss Kiane" Thomas, LGSW—
Owner Kiane Ink Healing in the Pen, LLC

"*Warrior Desire* is like an evening wearing that gold satin gown and going to a fancy ballet. There are moments of triumph, immense sadness, love and longing, and beautiful creativity. The conversation pieces are like the after-party where you drink champagne from crystal flutes and reflect on the beauty over rich conversation. A cathartic experience that leaves one knowing they have gone deeper into themselves, leaning into their essence, where they now look at the world through a lens that is a degree shinier and brighter. Quite the masterpiece. Cheers!

–Erica Sand, Author & Poet

Love Poems to Inspire Your
Fiercely Alive Whole Self

WARRIOR
DESIRE

To Jen
with Warrior Love
Laura

LAURA DI FRANCO

Warrior Desire
Love Poems to Inspire Your Fiercely Alive Whole Self
Laura Di Franco

DEDICATION

To the man who showed up in my life recently and ignited desires I never knew I had. Thank you for staying awake with me and all of my feelings, until all I had left was love.

THE POEMS

WARRIOR DESIRE is the inspired ache you feel when something tugs on your soul. It's the burning call of purpose and passion inside you.

Poems have moved through me since I was fifteen. It wasn't until much later in my life that I realized they were pieces of my soul moving their way through my heart to my pen and were meant to be written and read out loud and shared with the world.

Since that awakening, I've started to give them due justice by speaking them out loud to anyone who will listen, and even sharing on an open mic for the first time. Who knew that would heal me even more deeply?

The daily desire that dwells and grows in me, acting as fuel for this soul purging, is an energy ignited by alignment with purpose. The day I knew I was born to write, speak, and share my poems was the day everything changed. It was the day a magical, abundant, grateful and intensely joyful energy coursed through me and began driving my life and healing me from the inside out.

Since then I started attracting people into my life who mirror this energy. Who enhance it. Who match my vibration and desire. These people showed up in all areas of my life, including my love relationships.

Warrior Desire is not just wanting. And it's not only sexual, although the poems you'll read in this book certainly might turn you on in that way. Warrior Desire is the kind of feeling your body, mind, and soul can't ignore anymore. It's the kind meant to wake you up, make you question everything in your life, and move you with curiosity toward the things and people who light up your world with joy, love, and passion.

Warrior Desires are the sacred trail markers for a life lived fiercely alive, in love and joy. Are you following yours?

In this book you'll find love poems followed by questions. Take a few deep breaths, connect with your body, and clear your mind. Read the poem, and then the question. Allow yourself to dwell in the question itself and then if you're moved to, write what you feel. Let the words flow uncensored and free just for the sake of seeing what your soul has to say.

It's okay if your desire scares you a little. That's how you know it matters.

With big love,

Laura

ACKNOWLEDGMENTS

A huge thank you to the brilliantly talented Jeanette MacDonald who is the goddess behind the front cover artwork. Collaborating with you has been one of the biggest gifts. Thank you for being able to take my Warrior Desire description and put together something that I can't stop staring at. Find Jeanette at www.JeanetteMacDonaldArt.com.

Thank you to the men and women who've joined me at the open mic over the last year. Open mic therapy is real, and you all helped me stand up at the microphone enough times that I actually don't shake anymore.

Thank you to the souls who've listened to my poetry with bright eyes and deep, open hearts, and then, snapped, clapped, smiled, and hooted. Your enthusiastic responses live in me and fuel my writing every day.

Thank you to the people in my life who've inspired my poems. Whether it was love or pain I wrote through, I feel grateful.

Thank you to the 2014 class of John F. Barnes Myofascial Release Quantum Leap, and Jude Christensen for listening to the piece I wrote on the plane, helping me know I'm a poet, and for helping me believe my poems were worth sharing and reading out loud.

Thank you to Laura Munson, who after hearing one of my poems said, "I love simple poems; poems that cut straight to the heart." Those few healing words helped me give myself permission to write from my heart and never look back. My fear of not-good-enough was boring.

Thank you to Miss Kiane Thomas, who invited me to speak on her stage. My first poetry feature at Busboys & Poets in August of 2019 was a highlight of my poetic endeavors so far. I will always remember feeling like you trusted me and my poetry Kiane. I will never forget that.

Backpack Jeff, you said yes to coaching me, and for me it meant I was good enough. What you did for me went beyond sharpening my performance skills. Thank you.

To KaNikki Jakarta, thank you for what you do on that stage. Every time I hear you, or read your words, or attend your events I'm inspired. Every single time. Thank you for keeping the poetry fire burning in me always.

To my cover and interior book designer, Christy Collins. Thank you for making my books shine in a way I feel proud to share.

To my proofreader and fellow brave healer, Lori Calvo. Thank you for helping me with this book.

And to all the people who live in this world and feel poems all around them, thank you. Keep writing. Keep reading. Keep poetry close. And keep healing the world with your words.

SURRENDER

Find your way to my heart
sweet soul
Follow the light of my love
and let go

Tell me what's on your mind
my love
Release everything that binds
you down

I'm here to set you free
today
Help you to be you
and play

We're meant for bigger love
and now
I know I'm here to show
you how

We can have it all
and more
If you're ready to open
this sacred door

This door to my heart
is always yours
I've never wanted
anything more

Come on and be with me
the way
You know we
we're meant to stay

I'm awake in your arms
forever
Feel it in your bones
it matters

This is what we're made for
You're safe to stop and stay here
You'll find what you really want now
If you surrender to my love

Go ahead and surrender to my love
It's okay to surrender to my love

I'm waiting for you to surrender to my love
What if you could just surrender to my love?

During what I thought at first was a rebound relationship I discovered something interesting. I was the safe space for him to fall. Except his walls were so high I had to keep asking him to let me in. I had to keep asking him to surrender to what I was sure was something we both felt. I wrote a lot of poetry during the time I was discovering how to help him let go, and also what I truly wanted and needed in terms of love. Poetry was the way my desires expressed themselves when I had no other way to release. Love poems were my pressure relief.

What would it feel like to surrender to your deepest desires?

YOUR BODY IS A PLAYGROUND

Your body is a playground

Keeps me running around
chasing my heart
chasing my dreams
falling apart
thinking of things
I want to forget

Playing with you has me
catching my breath
again

Your body is a playground
keeps me running around
chasing my heart
chasing my dreams
falling apart
thinking of things
I want to forget

Waiting on you
has me feeling upset
again

Your body is a playground
every curve, up and down
how you smile
how you touch
let's talk a while
don't leave yet
we're just starting
ready set
go

Your body is a playground

There was a moment in time when I realized I didn't have to be ashamed of the way my body looked. I've spent most of my life wishing for another kind of body when it came to being intimate with someone, never feeling confident or free. Always inhibited and shy. Always hiding. Never really feeling good about what I saw in the mirror, when I was brave enough to look at myself naked.

The moment I finally felt free was after my love said the word, "Beautiful," about my naked body. In one simple word a lifetime's worth of uncertainty and dread washed away and I started to play.

When was the last time you played?

DROWN ME IN YOUR LOVE

Feel like I'm dying
after twenty years of trying
can't know
what's in store
for my soul

Crying like a child
wise but so wild
afraid to show
what my heart
can't ignore

I'm drowning in your love
drowning in your love
can't breathe
without a sign
from above

Lit from within
flirting with sin
I'm diving in
for the warmth
of your skin

Riding this wave
crashing hard
will you save me
your love's what I crave
all night and day

I'm drowning in your love
drowning in your love
can't breathe
without a sign
from above

Take me all night
I'll surrender and fly
giving in again
to the magic
in your hands

You're in control
I'm loving you more
you know
I can't just
walk out that door

I'm drowning in your love
drowning in your love
can't breathe
without a sign
from above

Please let me hold on
this dance's so fun
feel it all, it's real
I'll give you more
than what you need

I'll love you more
than what you need
you'll be high
when you realize
what you feel

I'm drowning in your love
can't walk away
I feel the pain
the way in and the way out
is your love

I'm drowning in your love
falling fast, falling deep
can't sleep til I know
you'll drown me
in your love

Please drown me in your love

There was a time I would have been embarrassed by this rather desperate-sounding poem. Today I read it and feel for that girl, in an older woman's body. It was like that teen-aged crush I had on the guy at the cabin at Clear Lake that one summer. All the feelings came crashing in. Some nights I'd call myself out and say, "Get a grip!" And some nights it would just consume me and I'd lay desperate and aching with tears rolling down my cheeks wondering if I'd ever feel worthy of someone's love.

What have you craved so deeply you felt like you were drowning without it?

Rest Your Body Down

Finding me
in you
slowly feeling you
in me
floating higher
I see
the only way
I could
ever be

Stars fall
for us
night shines
with us
reaching deeper
I find
the only place
I was
always me

Your eyes find
the way
to unwind me
your touch
my sigh
I can't imagine
another place
I'd rather
be

Rest your body down
on my soul
bring me to the end
don't go
wrap me up hard
with your love
make me know
I'll never want more.

Finally free
with you
feeling everything
I knew
breathing love
I can fly
my way
through
life

Dawn breaks
for us
another day
for us
dreaming bigger
I shake
my world
open
and play

Rest your body down
on my soul
bring me to the end

don't go
wrap me up hard
with your love
make me know
I'll never want more

Your love
makes its way
inside me
your rhythm
my light
I can't feel
more right
than
now

Music flows
for us
soul shows up
in us
pulling it all in
losing myself
in you
I create
something new

Come on now
touch me again
send me
to that place
I know
you can

I'm waiting
on fire
for your love

Rest your body down
on my soul
bring me to the end
don't go
wrap me up hard
with your love
make me know
I'll never want more

Make me know
I'll never want more

Please
make me know
I'll never want more

This was about wanting sex to feel like something bigger than physical. I'd experienced, for the first time in my life, someone who had me feeling lost in the now so deeply that everything else washed away. My senses tuned in to the moment in their entirety. Thinking stopped for a short while. Feeling led. And when I woke up from being so awake, I felt like maybe I'd been asleep. I had forgotten time.

What does it feel like to lose track of time?

I KNOW

I know about the magic
a love-wrapped, moon-dipped feel.

I know about the power
I'm ready to peel back the layers.

I know about the heartache
that goes along with this road.

I know there's no other path to take
if you wanna live like there's no tomorrow.

I'm ready for a sign
I'm ready, it's time
I'm going all the way
Don't ask me to stay stuck in this place
I'll fade away.

I know about the pain
but I'm not willing to play this game

I know what's keeping me chained
but I'm breaking free today.

I know about the way
evil grabs hold of your mind.

I know all the secrets
to busting through this fucked up jail.

I'm ready for a sign
I'm ready, it's time

I'm going all the way
Don't ask me to stay stuck in this place
I'll fade away.

Take me down
Take me now
Take me gently
I'm ready to fall.

I know about the joy
the light-filled, sweet-tasting sky.

I know about the courage it takes
and I'm ready to fight.

I know about the sunrise
the burning red desire.

I know how to fly
I'm ready to make love my home.

I'm ready for a sign
I'm ready, it's time
I'm going all the way
Don't ask me to stay in this place
I'll fade away.

Take me down
Take me now
Take me gently
I'm ready to fall.

I want it all
I want it now
You can't stop
this sacred waterfall.

I'm ready for a sign
I'm ready, it's time
I'm going all the way
Don't ask me to stay stuck in this place
I'll fade away.

I'll fade away.

I know about the darkness
what lurks in the shadows tonight.

I know how to channel my soul
blast it all with the light.

I know how to call on love
make a life worth living.

I know all the secrets
to keep myself free from the Hell.

I want it all
I want it now
You can't stop
this sacred waterfall.

Don't ask me to stay stuck in this place
I'll fade away.

The idea that we can't know big love without knowing big sorrow is something that throws me off course some days. I get the yin yang of life. I have the perspective I need. And now that I know both ends, I choose love.

What darkness have you endured because you knew it meant you'd feel the light?

Dancing With Fire

I rest my soul
in the trees
surrender my thoughts
to the breeze
floating higher
I see
this is the way
I was meant to be,
free.

I lay down my truth
beneath the sky
let go of my doubts
with a sigh
buzzing louder
I feel
everything I'm supposed
to feel.

Leaving my past
with the stars
giving up the last
of my scars
soaring closer
I know
how to make love
to the light.

I'm closer
to the sky
don't care about knowing
the whys
staying here
I can breathe
I can finally breathe
again.

I lay down my weapons
and pray
ask to be shown
the way
grateful
to play
for a moment
with true soul.

I dance with fire
in the dark
take the risk
with my heart
my body knows
this's how
it was meant
to feel.
free.

I ended up writing a lot about feeling free in my body during the time I realized I could play more and worry less. It was new to me to feel confident about that. It was new to me to not feel dirty or ashamed. I had to re-identify with the woman who was emerging and get even more comfortable in that new skin, literally. The freedom cracked me open, and I still feel the full amount of long-term, pent-up rage waiting for its day to be released. In the meantime, I leave the cap off and give it an escape route if and when it needs one. I pay attention to the days I feel like I'm constricting again.

How does it feel to be free in your body?

BREATHLESS

You leave me breathless
can't catch this
feeling
I'm wanting
all the time now
that you're
with me.

I'm begging you
to touch this
place
I'm wanting
more and more.

Please
put your hands on me
slide them down gently
go slower
wait there until I can't breathe
find it
there you go
slower still
until the stars light up the sky
and I'm flying.

You leave me painless
can't hold this
feeling
I'm needing
all the time now

that you're
near me.

I'm always asking you
to love
the way
you do that makes
me burn like fire
oh yes
now

Put your hands on me
slide them down gently
go slower
wait there until I can't breathe
find it
there you go
slower still
until the stars light up the sky
and I'm flying.

I'm flying
breathless
holding on to bliss
a moment more
waiting for you
to meet me there
and you're there.

Hold me here
a little longer
keep me rolling

a little softer
wrap me a little tighter
come a little closer
breathe a little deeper.

Put your hands on me
slide them down gently
go slower
wait there until I can't breathe
find it
there you go
now slower still
until the stars light up the sky
and I'm flying.

When have you ached so deeply you couldn't catch your breath?

GOOD MORNING NIGHT

Nightbirds twill
in
full moonlight.
Bright magic
alive
in dark mist
weeks before
fireflies.

Resting
in deep sighs
the sky
guides me home,
air still dry
and cool
through my lungs.

Wondering why
three a.m. calls
again
like a bugle;
dreamy heart
alert,
poem-breathing soul
sure as day.

But it's always
the night
whispering
my name,

playing games,
changing
my mind
about things like
who I am.

Why not write
then,
I muse
beginning to peck
these words.
And they come
and come
from
the twill
and the light
and the mist
in a trumpet
solo
having me smelling coffee
way
too
early.

My eyes
decide
they'll try closing
again
as
one morning bird
announces
the sun.

I blink
unbelieving
of time.
I still see moonlight
on the other side
of light-pink-orange
hues.

Same sky
different sigh.
Good morning
night.
Time for you to
run along.
I have coffee
and
sunrise
has stolen
your show
for now.

What time of day or night turns you on the most?

BAREFOOT

I like to ride
bareback on horses
barefoot,
mane in my hands,

walk over warm, pink
sands
on a beach hidden
from view.

I like to drive fast
hugging corners
with special tires
feel the pull in my abs,

climb rocks
a little too big
sweating from
the task.

I like to taste chocolate
with my nose
and my soul
before my tongue,

have a little too much fun
dancing
and make a laughing moan
when the lights come on.

I like to wear black silk
underwear
beneath my sweats
and call it my uniform,

worship unicorns
lapis lazuli
Gabriel
and Pasta Fazool.

I like sex
in the shower
and hours of
laying around spent and naked.

I'll take a little
afternoon nap
and an unexpected dream
midday.

I like when poems come
in the middle of silence
like a tiny spark in a cave
lighting the way to my soul,

and days with enough snow
that nothing's a go
and I can rest into life
and just be.

Connecting with all of the things that turn me on was part of the way I healed. I had to give myself permission to make joy a priority. To allow desires to drive my actions each day. And poems were one of the ways those nuggets of soul poured out and made themselves witnessed.

What makes you feel sexy?

She's Better Like That

I walk
with a river raging inside me
and she's hungry.
Always
hungry.
I feed her heart
and soul
and peanuts sometimes.
Occasionally I forget
she needs to breathe.
The quiet hours come
and she rages
harder
louder;
more anxious
to carve her path
in the stones of my life.
She rises
with the storms.
She's almost better
like that;
running like a maniac,
spilling over the edges,
keeping up with
a faster pace
of flow.
And when she reaches that place
of calm;
no boulders to impress,
no boundaries to push,

she looks around
curious,
like she's supposed to be carving,
or rushing
or spilling over.
She tries breathing.
She tries on
the calm.
But it just doesn't fit.
She was born the river
and was meant to
run
and rage
and flow like a wild fire
out of control
and magnificent.
She's better like that.

There was a point that I just stopped fighting being me. The full-on me. The crazy, wild, sexy, and too-much me. There was a point I realized I was spending too much energy thinking things about how I shouldn't this, or shouldn't that. All the while it would have been so much easier to just be me. I watch myself with way more compassion now. And I make it okay no matter what I see. I see with awareness and understanding. I try not to judge myself too much.

When do you feel the most wild you? Can you let her out?

I Can Wait a Little Longer

I wake
as the bed shakes
and you finally
come to bed.

I back into the spoon
the same moment
your arm reaches
over my top thigh
to my bottom hip
to tuck me in.

This one move
creates the deepest
exhale.

Feeling the warmth of your front
on my back,
the shape of yours
fitting into mine
gets me high
and I close my eyes
to hear you sigh.

The night
just stills
through
to my soul.

Sweet dreams
are born
in this moment.

The breath I take
makes everything
okay.

I drift into you
and can wait
a little longer
for
tomorrow.

What moment could you linger in forever?

SOMETHING SO GOOD

Last night I cried
in your arms.
You felt the drops
on your chest,
noticed the change
in my breath.
You knew,
and waited quietly.
"Everything okay?"
you finally whispered
as I continued to try
to choke it all down,
afraid you'd think
something bad.
"I could crawl inside and stay forever," I barely
said,
"I feel something so big."
"It's not bad," I reassured.
"I know," you replied,
and placed your smooth warm hands
on that place on my back
cradling my tears
until they were dry.

I've been lucky enough to spend time with someone who lets me be myself, even in my full emotions. I've noticed how he waits. I've noticed how the emotions don't bother him and how he's able to just be with it. What this did for me was allow me to heal, without words. This allowed me to shed the healing tears without having to have an explanation, or fixing. His patience was the space I needed. I was able to come to the places I needed to on my own. The room he allowed my soul to breathe in felt like a miracle to me.

When did love move you to tears?

You're the Reason

Wrapped inside
your love
for the first time
I'm feeling
safe
a shield
made of essence
of presence
surrounds me
protects me
breathes life
through me
new tastes
play on my tongue
in my heart
permeate
my soul
I'm a fool
for you
you know
I'm melted
open wide
aching
all the time
new touch
sends ripples
over skin
and sin
dissolves
in bliss

your kiss
brings me here
straight
to my core
leaving me
full
glowing
overflowing
and ready
for more love
able to receive
for the first time
able to feel
what love
means
held in
your strength
I find mine
I'm high
with you
fly
with you
I'm certain
I'll die
knowing you
are the reason
I know how it feels
to be wild
and alive.

When did you feel totally safe?

LOVE ME THAT HARD

Love me so hard
I lose my breath.
Surprise me.
Pull out
that shy smile.
Kiss me again.
Tell me things
I'll never forget.
Things nobody else
has said.
Delight me with
a different tone.
Laughter so long
I groan.
An adventure
I wasn't expecting.
A hug that
never ends.
Touch me
there.
Linger and breathe.
Make me know
you see,
and feel.
Make me wonder
who you are.
Love me so hard
my faith returns
and I'm excited
to learn more.

Do things
that wake me up.
Force me
to take notice.
Catch me
from behind
and slowly
pull me in.
Make my skin
buzz.
Make me believe
in something.
Tell me a story
of your life.
Cry.
Let me touch
your heart.
Show me you're
part human.
Start a new hobby
with my soul.
Dance and sing
until wings
grow from my back.
And the sky
seems ready
to hand me the stars.
Surprise me.
Love me that hard.

What surprises you about love?

Make it Real

Let I love you
fall from your lips.
There's no trick,
just say it
if she matters that much.

I like you a lot
is fifth-grade talk.
It won't fly
for the sweet, wild woman
you got.

Touch her with words,
light her soul on fire.
Be brave,
say the thing
she's longing to hear.

Be clear about it now,
time to be out loud.
Whisper if you must
but trust
what you feel.

Here's the deal about love,
it's aching to grow big.
What it needs most
is folks
who aren't afraid to dig deep.

Sow seeds with your voice,
let her hear what's inside.
You've got a choice, don't hide
let her know
everything she means.

Let your love dance through,
make the sounds.
Stop fooling around,
get to the vibration
she needs.

Sometimes the action
is taking a step.
Risk your heart,
fall apart, be afraid
say it anyway.

Move your love
from your heart to your tongue.
Through the lump in your throat
and the hole in your soul
to her face just for once.

Maybe this move
is just what you need.
You'll see
everything will change
when you make this real.

Look at her now,
let your eyes talk first.

Then find the courage
say, "I love you babe,
you're the light in my day."

"You're everything I need,
you're more than I could hope.
Being with you feels good
I want more of this food
for my soul."

"I love you more than you know.
This is real.
I want you to know.
Don't want to live another day
without telling you so."

At this point I was comfortable with "I love you," and he wasn't. And then I started to question everything. I started to understand his trauma. His fears. I started to wonder if what I felt was the same as what he did. I was suddenly unsure. All because of those three little words.

When is it hard to say the words, "I love you?"

It Can Be Like This

Your body's my elixir
It's safe to say
I can't get enough
of your sweet touch.

Inhaling your vibes
calm and strong
brings me down
a notch.

And my soul lays back
and floats.

Your tone
shakes my bones
awake.

My skin comes alive
in the wake
of your lips
over my face.

The way you laugh
lifts my heart.
She smiles inside;
spouts wings out her back
and she soars
to meet yours,
stumbling around
with words

unsure
and shy.

Cuz she's never met
a guy
who's given her heart
wings before.

Never been with a man
who made her feel
sure
about love
until now.
Never realized
it could be
like this.

Bliss.

Relaxed kiss.

Moments to cherish
instead of regret.

A fire of hope
burning for bigger
badder
juicier
love.

It can be
like this.

Oh yes
It can be like this.

I started to feel excited about love being different than I'd experienced before. I started to feel excited that the feeling was bigger than anything in my life so far. And I couldn't quite put the words to the feels. All I knew at this point was that I was smiling way more than frowning. And that for a couple of decades prior to that, it was the other way around.

When do you feel the most alive?

You Are My Haven

You are my haven,
my safe space to be
me.

You're my shelter
in a storm.
The only one
who sees.

You feed
my soul,
wrap your arms
around my heart,
hold the pieces
broken apart.
You
are the glue.

You're the mirror
for my soul
how I know
myself
my essence
my purpose
my worth,
get acquainted
with the light
and the dark.

You help me
shine
remind me
there's no more time
to be afraid.

What you say
sits softly
in my core
twirling
a magic wand
creating a song
from the shadows
there.

Finding you
like a jewel
just lying there
all sparkly and blue
in the mud
saying, "scoop me up."
It's like you
were dropped there
from heaven.

My haven
is you,
the calm
the fire
the peace

you inspire
the strength
I feel
in my bones
how my mind
feels light
and free.

Thank you
for giving those treasures
to me.
Thank you for
treading
gently,
holding me
firmly,
keeping me
still,
forcing me
into
the healing.

You
are my haven.

When has someone felt like a haven to you?

When Our Eyes Talk

When our eyes talk
and our fingers kiss
tell me
it's not bliss

When the heat between
drips our worries clean
and everything seems
right

You'll find me there
as our dreams meet
and I stare
into your soul

When our hearts beat
together
the rhythmic rise of our breath
is another world

When your energy
envelops me
I dance free
inside your embrace

You'll find me here
aching for you
when our eyes talk
and you say, "I'm yours."

When my essence hears
your whisper
a soft plea
calling me home

When your tone
vibrates through my world
my petals unfurl
I'm full blown

You'll find me waiting
puppy-dog-eyed
but warrior-souled
ready for your love

When our eyes talk
I hear everything
I feel everything
I'm meant to feel.

Can you read someone's eyes?

STAY RIGHT THERE

Stay right there
sit still
let me unbuckle your belt
pop that snap
slide your zipper down
slow.
Close your eyes
don't touch me
yet.
Breathe me in.
Feel my
vibration.
Let me slide my hands
inside,
touch you,
make you rise
to meet me.
Let me
pull your tee
up over your chest,
mouth on skin
as I go
collar bone
to belly button
missing nothing
in between.
Wait.
Keep your hands
to yourself
just a little while

longer.
Let me taste
the skin
on your hips,
feel
the power
of your thighs,
make my own self
rise
unconfined,
throw my dress
to the side
and slide myself
over the top
of you,
douse you
in fire
until your eyes
widen
and desire
brings your hands
to my waist.
Pull me closer
let your soul
be the place
touching me
while your fingers
trace
the small of my back.
Let me hear
your moan
a soft

whisper
behind my ear
pulling goosebumps
up
and down
my neck.
Don't hold back now.
Meet my pace
my rhythm
watch my face
for signs
I'm close
listen for the
sigh
I'm there
don't stop
keep yourself
here
til the end.
Send me off
with the delight
of your release
pull me in
hard
caress
breath
dripping
mess
sigh
lingering
pulse
fly off

into dreamy sleep
forget
rest.
Stay right there.

By this time there were a lot of love poems moving through me. And I was afraid to share many of them. I'd been writing erotic stories as well. And nobody was ever going to read them, was my fear. I was finding the permission I needed to feel sensual and sexual. And for a while, it was words on my pages for only me (and sometimes him) to read.

What desires feel difficult to talk about?

Naked Chocolate

Watching you sleep
naked chocolate
over creamy sheets
breathing deep
I let myself go
write poems
realize
I know
why my soul aches
why it takes
all of me
to love you.

When does it take all of you to love?

A Heap of Sweat and Fire

Keep your lips on mine.
Your kiss speaks.
Those luscious things
between your cheeks
warm and soft
hold me still,
a little drunk.
That Mmmm
the hum they pull
from my soul
vibrates on my tongue,
teases it out
to suck
inhale your taste
fill my nose
with sweet vapors
you make.
Wait
keep me here.
Let me play
longer.
Surrender
your face.
Sink deep in my embrace.
Don't rush.
Be hushed by my mouth.
Let your hands speak,
your sighs
the only sounds.
Eyes closed

feel more
let me in
fall open.
Turn the furnace up
with your quiet,
slow, gentle touch.
Keep me burning
until we come
together
exhausted
in a heap of sweat
and fire.
And then let me kiss you a little more.

When have you felt lost in love?

I Think You Meant Me

You touched me.
I looked at my feet.
You said,
"Beautiful."
I think you meant me.
My worth
rose to the surface,
peeked her head out.
I doubted.
Past pain
played a game
with my mind.
You were kind
anyway.
You listened.
You touched me again.
My eyes
met yours this time.
And we kissed
for a thousand miles.

What do you need to hear to help you feel worthy of your desires?

The Next Move

I ride waves of uncertainty
without a boat
I'm soaked
heavy
ready to let go

I fight against the current
without a chance
the resistance
thick
with habit

I can't swim
dark waters
box me in
black
shivering

I dream of dying
without caring
I'm done
trying
for love

I'm tired of hurting
for someone
not going
in my direction
expecting different

Flat on my back
staring
chest tearing apart
breaking
with ache

Yet I still wake
with a dream
my life's at stake
hope makes it's way
in

I trust I'm here
for a reason
but I'm tired
spent
bleeding

Show me the way
to something
worth it
make me believe
in myself

Hold my hand
and drag me
show me love
tell me
it's real

Steal my heart
pet my soul
don't take me
for a
fool

I ride waves
with angels
I'm soaked
in sacred
purpose

I hang with wizards
party with witches
make love with Gods
play with Goddesses
I am love

I am love
damnit
don't pretend
you can't see
my divinity

Test me again
with doubt
try fear and shame
some blame
it's all a game

And I'm a warrior
I slay pain
eat fear for breakfast
mastered the game
I'm ready for the next move.

Seems life had more heartbreak in store for me. And funny how I realized in the moments that felt like pure despair, just how far away from deep passion I was in my last relationship. The deeper level of pain woke me to my numbed up past. And I then had to decide whether or not I was made for that deeper kind of pain. Whether or not I'd still want to play the game, knowing there might only be a deeper level waiting for me. But of course I stayed the path, because warriors do that.

What's your next move after heartache?

Worth Everything

You didn't hug me last night
didn't soften my pain
say the thing
I longed to hear.
I waited for hours
hoping you'd
come around,
left to the darkness
of my mind
again.

You didn't put down your phone
or reach over to let me know
you were there.
I ached for your stare
but you let the glow
hypnotize you
again
while my heart
shriveled and cooled.

You didn't try to feel.
Explained it all away instead
making it seem
not real
making me think I'm a fool.
I waited for something new
something true
something more.
It didn't come.

You didn't say the words
you know, the ones too much to say
the words I crave to let play
in my soul.
I waited
ears perked
arms of my heart wide.
You walked right by
mumbled something
about next year.

I let you in without a thought
without a flicker
of doubt.
I trusted my heart.
I keep opening the door
waiting for you to walk in
from the cold.
You stand there
waiting for an invitation
when my smile
should be all you need.

It's not going to be
like this much longer
I'd love to tell you
I'm stronger
than this
but every girl
has limits
and you're testing mine.

This time I'm flying without you
unless you grow your wings too.

You didn't tell me
you couldn't love
didn't warn me your wound
might be deeper than mine
didn't find the time
to help me understand
the gravity
against which you stand
constantly proving yourself
to the world.

You should have hugged me last night
whispered I love you in my ear
felt everything I have to give
told me how it helps you live
walked through that door
scooped me in your arms
and made me know
I'm safe
soul-embraced
worth your time
worth the pain
worth everything.

You should have hugged me last night.

What won't you stand for anymore?

THE BEST GOOD MORNING

Ever linger
in bed
eyes closed
fully awake
feel the warmth
held in the sheets
your bodies made
the night before.
Pull the covers
up
back into
the spoon
notice
he's very awake
too.
Feel the ache
open your legs
and invite him in
again.
Ever lay there
and think
it's a dream
it feels so good
wrapped
in his skin
arms
legs
his face
nuzzling yours
hot breath

puffing
on your neck
making shivers
run your spine.
This time
it's not
a dream.
He moves slow
knows
what to do.
For once
you're lost
in the best
"Good morning"
of your life.

What's your best good morning?

THE WAY YOU TAKE CARE OF ME

It's not the money
or the clothes
I need.
Not any thing
you give me.
The way you take care of me
floats in waves
across my face
when gratitude dances
around my soul
pinking my cheeks,
singing her song
like nobody's watching.

It spreads
like wildfire
through my eyes
watching you try
to help me
be me,
not judging the way
I move myself
with too much passion
through this world.

The way you take care of me
wraps around my heart
like a long-lost friend
at the airport
crying tears of
love

and missed embrace.
Only your hands
always find
exactly the right time
to move around my waist
like they know,
like they feel
my vibration
from the other room.

The way you take care of me
stands its ground
when I go insane
making up
some game to play
to escape
how I feel.
It sits solid
gold
a stone temple
in my world,
worshiping you
is a daily refuge
for my wild
warrior love.

The way you take care of me
spins and twirls
over my skin,
leaving raspberry-glitter trails
of laughter
about nothing
or everything,

helping me remember
my purpose
reclaim
my worth
play catch
with my little girl again.

I feel her bright
hazel eyes
look up
at the sky,
make shapes
from the clouds,
dream up
a million things
before noon
when I'm with you.

The way you take care of me
whispers sweet
melodies
in my ear
helps me believe
in myself
stands clear
of negativity
reaching for promise
hope
and possibility.

I love the way
you take care of me
how you

being you
automatically
helps me
be me
unapologetically
enthusiastically
miraculously brave
with an unstoppable
mission
to feel illegal amounts
of joy.

Stay right there
and take care of me
just the way you do.
Keep inviting me
into the playground
where your love
sits on the swings
beckoning me
on the ride
of my life.
Free
hair-flying
delight.
Lets say we'll do that
forever
and a day,
and I promise
to take care of you
too.

How do you feel taken care of?

I Love You Too

Resting on his back
I straddled his waist,
gentle hands held my sides.
I hovered there
pulling the last few
deep breaths into my lungs.

Drawing my hair to the side
I nestled down
into his chest,
one arm around his low back
one around his neck,
my legs like vines
around his.

"Sometimes, I can be this close,"
I whispered,
"And still want to be closer."
"Sometimes I want to crawl inside,"
I said,
"And disappear,"
A deeply stuck cry
set free from my throat.

Lodged there for weeks
his energy was the key
to releasing it.
"You must think I'm crazy,"
I said.
"I know you're crazy,"

he said.
I laughed softly in his ear.

He held me gently
caressing my skin
until my nose stuffed up.
I rolled off to grab tissues,
felt him rearranging himself
in the sheets behind me.
We settled into
a warm spoon.

So much to say.
And the silence;
a refuge,
like the strong
cradle of his body.
I let myself stay there
drifting off.

"You worry too much,"
he offered softly.
"Don't worry so much,"
he said to the silence.
"Okay," was all I had.
I knew it wouldn't be easy.

I love you, I said
in my mind,
hoping he'd feel it

so I wouldn't have to
say it out loud.
He reached his arm
across my body
and tucked me closer in.
I think that was
his "I love you too."

In this relationship I've spent much of my time convincing myself that actions speak louder than words. Those are always his words when I ask about saying the words "I love you." And I believed him for a long time. Because his actions were most always palpable, when it came to love. And yet there's a part of me that still needs to hear it. I'm not sure why I need that. But I do. And I've come to a point in my life where I'm okay needing what I need. And I'm okay asking for that. But "I love you," always seems bigger and scarier somehow.

How do you say I love you without words?

To Be Together

You're black
I'm white
when we're face to face
instead of fright
I feel love.
Eyes closed
fast embrace
instead of doubt
I feel sure.
Sure color
doesn't matter
when more important things
wait
for our attention
our energy
our undeniable
connection.
I'm short
you're tall
yet you never
make me feel small
only protected.
My heart's
in your gentle hands.
My soul
sings
as you listen.
I'm wise
you're young

an old soul
arriving again
to teach
to guide
to awaken
stir evolution
in my bones.
I'm ready
you're unsure
doesn't stop
our purpose
mistakes
just the way
we grow together.
I'm afraid
but not because
you're different
than me
but because we only have
this short time
to love
to live
to be
together.

Being with someone younger than me has been a healing journey all on its own. There's a constant test to my self-esteem, even though I thought I nailed that sucker long ago. It's been interesting. Most days age, color, height, or anything else I see as different, isn't a factor. It's never up in my mind as anything noticeable. Because connection is all that really matters. And a strong connection, when you feel that, overpowers any of the things society has taught us is a problem between two people in love. And society is really the bigger issue. What I'm willing to be in front of others. I'm asking myself again today...what are you willing to be in the name of this love you feel?

How does being different bring you together?

There With You

I sit in deep water
tilting my head
just far back enough to breathe.
I'm standing up
but nobody sees.
Only I know
how the cold murkiness
feels.
I stand for the things
I never could before,
my story silently crouched
in a safe corner
of my heart
keeping so silent
you'll never know
she's there.

I stand by myself
treading
balancing
in the seaweed
avoiding being strangled
thinking I'm feeling
sharks,
planning the way
I'll survive.
I fight
invisible monsters
and mostly win.

Sometimes I'm out
to chest level
and it feels so warm
and good.

You can't see
underneath.
You don't feel
my fight.
But once in a while
you speak words
of delight
and they're like
soft tiny kisses
for my soul.
Once in a while
I know I'm meant
to be.
Once in a while
I don't feel
like I'm drowning.

So please
keep shining your light
on me.
Please
whisper your words
again.
Please know
every single time
you reach for my hand

you pull me out
a little bit more
and I soar there
with you.
I'm me there with you.
Everything's right and true
there with you.

This one is meant for someone you call your lover or some-one you call your friend. When someone is loving the whole you, the imperfect you, the full-of-mistakes-and-failures you, hold on to that person for dear life. You're lucky if you get one person in this lifetime that helps you feel that way; loved with all of your faults. I'm lucky to have had a few people in my life who help me feel loved for all of who I am.

Do you ever lose yourself with another person?

I'll Burn Forever

I love the way
you light my soul on fire
how my dreams ignite
the stars inside my mind
collide
my world blows apart
possibilities simmer
underneath my skin
sizzling and popping
in a heated dance
a chance to feel
everything bigger
better
softer.
Your presence
feathers
over my thighs
tickling the bluest
blazing skies
in hues seeping
from my fingertips
back over to you
the purple flame
shining from my eyes
grazing your smile
pulling in the secrets
your dimples keep
memorizing how your lips
meet

impossibly cute smirking
playing a strip-tease
around me.
I ache for the weight
of your chest
holding me down
the sound of your breath
the next time
you say my name
whisper your truth
blow shivers through
my spine
and how our bodies
seem to rhyme
together.
I love the crave
keeping my days
full
how joy stays
unshakable
through our mistakes
how play is the means
by which we make
our love
how ease finds a path
through this house
every
single
day.
I love the way I feel
with you and me
at the wheel

lost in bliss
your kiss
melting me
all over the place
joy overwhelming
uncertainty
peace soothing
smoothing out edges
of doubt
and fear
how sharp bites
catching me by surprise
no longer keep
me in the pit
cuz I'm lit
so bright
from within
with you by my side.
Love of my life
my fire guy
I'll always know
your gift
I'll die with a smile
with this
time you've spent
cracking open my heart
teaching me
fearless things
singing me to sleep
with your sweet
melodies
old soul answers

pulling truth
from my tongue
keeping body mind
young
in touch
with fun
never ending love
eternity the keeper
of this story
love's biggest lesson
learned.
I love the way
you light my soul on fire
I'll burn forever
with your love.

What's the deepest love you've ever experienced?

WILD DESIRE

I notice where the summer breeze
touches my skin
and I begin
to come alive

where sun beams
warm my face
no trace
of want or worry

tweets and twitters
flutter through my mind
the world becomes kind
in sacred spaces...

breath is hot
bothered
passion rises
surprising my tired soul

high from staring
at cloud-covered skies
drifting pictures
making love to my eyes

noticing how a moment
holds everything I need
to feel a deep
desperate fire

wild desire
reaches out
dancing bare
teasing intolerable dare

play with me
she whispers
behind my ear
sending shivers everywhere.

How do you experience desire?

The Vibration of Love

from the sacred moonlit night
she rose
from the soft pink sunrise
she rose
from the warm, rugged earth
she rose
from her soul's flaming essence
she rose
and ignited a revolution
brave
worthy
out loud
purposeful
positive
generous
and aware...
she rose, lit from within
shining out
feeling everything
healing everything
living the joy
honoring the pain
touching stillness
allowing the vibration
of love
to rule.

The more I gave myself permission to let the energy and vibration of love to be my priority, the more energy I felt, the healthier I felt, and the more it seems I have to give every single day. I prioritize joy. After one of my writing classes a student asked me, "How do you have so much energy?" "I prioritize joy," I replied, somewhat surprised that slipped out of my mouth so easily. But it was true. And I made it a little more real by being brave enough to say it out loud.

How do you raise your vibration?

I'm Living for This

A moment
lost in time
sublime in taste
color...sound
fully cracked open
found
I grabbed hands with my soul
and danced
felt the trance
of light
and love
kissed by bliss
wrapped in this
moment
only
taken
lost
weightless
alive.
I'm living for this.

What do you live for?

SHATTERED

My heart's caught in your trap
coming apart
moving through the spaces between the wires
cutting off pieces to fit through
bleeding for you
needing to know you want me too

I'm shattered and raw
crawling
barely breathing down in that space near the
ground
where they say there's air
but only despair
sits down there with my soul

I'm smart enough to know I'll escape
playing this game
I know the moves I've played a thousand times
shutting down inside
pretending I don't feel
trying to hide myself from the world

I'm good enough to remember a different way
breaking wide open
letting the cracks fill with light
splitting further is how I'll fight
believing in bigger things
even though this stings

I know I'll survive feeling this fucking alive
a full unraveling
no longer interested in finding the old pieces
falling into the same patterns
keeping it all together
no...I'm better when I'm shattered

"I'm better when I'm shattered," speaks to the courage to feel. Because when I allow myself to feel everything it means I get to feel the good stuff too. I get to have a taste of illegal amounts of joy and what that feels like. I get to taste bliss and talk about what that feels like. The more I allow my heart to break, and not try to stuff that pain, the more I feel what "totally shattered" feels like, the more I open a space for what else is possible. And that what else is so good. So when I'm feeling pain most times I do try to talk myself into feeling all of it. Because I know the prize.

What good comes from being shattered?

MAYBE TONIGHT

Wasting time
stuck in my mind
when I could be
loving you harder

Afraid my heart
will break apart
so I keep my thoughts
quiet

When will I see
this aint' for me
a warrior
speaks her soul

How can I be
brave and free
tell you all
you need to know

Maybe today
you'll hear me say
I love you
you're my world

Maybe tonight
I'll lay beside you
let bliss
be my guide

Maybe tomorrow
I'll let doubt go
be sure
of what I feel

Maybe someday
I'll make way
for the truth
of my desires

Until then
I'll use my pen
write rhymes
I hope you'll read

Until then
I'll wake up again
plant seeds
to grow strong

While you wait
try to be patient
everything's about
to change

Loving you
is moving me through
the fear
and the shame

Loving you
feels like truth

and I'm willing
to change the game

Listen tonight
when I stop the fight
whisper softly
from my core

I love you so much
you light me up
I'm yours forever
and a little more

Speaking up and feeling worthy to do so has been the theme of the kind of brave I've had to practice in my life. I'm no longer interested in how that started, who I might blame for it, or what reasons I still feel triggered. With awareness I either make a choice to speak, or not. With awareness I now take responsibility for my own heart. And with awareness I choose, more and more, to speak the words of my soul; to choose that healing.

What thoughts keep you from speaking your heart out loud?

I Love Getting Lost

I love getting lost in a poem
connecting with words moving through me
from a mysterious and wonderful place,
catching them with my pen
in the quiet hours
when sounds are only my breath
and heartbeat
and the scribble of ink on the page.

I love writing and reading them out loud
hearing their rhythm and rhyme
feeling their sting
or the pang they make
against my heart
when it recognizes itself in a word
or a scene.

I love the way I feel when a poem comes
and someone says, "I love this!"
I'm in love with their reaction,
the sparkle in their eyes
or if I'm lucky, their applause
only when I'm brave enough
to stand up and share the things my soul speaks.

When poems fly free from me
I love them more than most all other
every day things
so much so I wonder what I'm doing

writing things like blogs and books
and other words
with less fire in them.

I love getting lost in a poem
stoking the flame in my soul
teasing out the sparks
delighting in the dance they do
on my skin
in goosebumps
and shivers.

I love how a poem lives
in the corners of my mouth
and the light beams through the blind slats
in the wanting ache between my thighs
or the blue of the October sky
the long sigh
that escapes when I'm relaxed.

I love getting lost in a poem.

How or where do you love being lost?

About You

I sit to write a poem
about you
wrap my words around the feel
of your arms wrapped around my waist,
your taste on my tongue,
your place in the story of my life.

I make words that say what I mean when I say
I love you,
for real this time,
be out loud about the void in my soul
you filled
the first day your eyes smiled
and my heart moved toward the front of my
chest a little more
to meet you.

I find the flow in knowing
bigger love waited
for me to wake up and be it
so I could give it.

When I spit my drink
from the laughter spewing from my mouth
from that same joke you like to tell
over and over
I realized that joy had settled
deep within me
and it wasn't going anywhere soon.
And that felt really, really good.

Who's your poem about?

Dear Warrior,

The more you honor your desires, the more fiercely alive you'll feel. We are all wired for desire. We move through life, inspired because of it. The natural flow of desire is something to notice, respect and cherish.

I hope you enjoyed these poems and that you'll pick a few to read out loud. Savor the feels they conjure up and give yourself permission to dwell in the desire they evoke in you. I highly encourage you to fill the blank spaces with your own words and poems. And if you have one you'd like to share with me, send it to bewarriorlove@gmail.com I might even share it on my poetry page.

With Warrior Love,
Laura

P.S. come play with me on my poetry page on Facebook: www.Facebook.com/WarriorLove

You'll find my previous Warrior Journal titles on Amazon.com

BraveHealer.com is where you'll find me and my writing and healing services.

YourHighVibeBiz.com is where you'll find a new community for entrepreneurs that is changing the world.

I can't wait to connect with you!

Other books by Laura Di Franco

Poetry

Warrior Love, A Journal to Inspire Your Fiercely Alive Whole Self

Warrior Joy, A Journal to Inspire Your Fiercely Alive Whole Self

Warrior Soul, A Journal to Inspire Your Fiercely Alive Whole Self

Warrior Dreams, A Journal to Inspire Your Fiercely Alive Whole Self

Teaching Memoir

Living, Healing and Tae Kwon Do, A Memoir to Inspire Your Inner Warrior

Brave Healing, A Guide for Your Journey

Co-Authored Projects

Winning in Life and Work: Dare to Dream

What's in Your Web, Stories of Fascial Freedom

365 Ways to Connect With the Soul

Superwoman Myths, Break the Rules of Silence and Speak Up Your Truth

More about the Author

Laura has a third-degree black belt and a clear preference for traveling fast and being badass. She is also the pragmatic champion of small business owners who want to push their health-based practices to the next level but need a little help to do so.

Through her Bethesda-based Brave Healer Productions, Laura offers inspiring speeches, spoken word poetry, workshops, an online writing club, and other services that can help talented health professionals tell their own stories so they too can maximize their professional impact. Laura has a built a powerful community of brave healers who are learning to spread their message of health and empowerment in much bigger ways.

With almost three decades of expertise in holistic physical therapy behind her, she has written eight books including the aptly titled *Brave Healing, a Guide for Your Journey*. Shouldn't Laura be helping you with your journey? Learn more at BraveHealer.com and YourHighVibeBiz.com

Your words will heal the world when you're brave enough to share them.

Made in the USA
Middletown, DE
24 November 2019

79318500R00080